Sabrir

CW00540064

Bloomsbury Methuen Drama
An imprint of Bloomsbury Publishing Plc

B L O O M S B U R Y
LONDON • NEW DELHI • NEW YORK • SYDNEY

Bloomsbury Methuen Drama
An imprint of Bloomsbury Publishing Plc

Imprint previously known as Methuen Drama

50 Bedford Square	1385 Broadway
London	New York
WC1B 3DP	NY 10018
UK	USA

www.bloomsbury.com

Bloomsbury is a registered trade mark of Bloomsbury Publishing Plc

First published 2015

© Sabrina Mahfouz, 2015

British Library Cataloguing-in-Publication Data
A catalogue record for this book is available from the British Library.

ISBN: PB: 978-1-4742-6539-3
ePub: 978-1-4742-6541-6
ePDF: 978-1-4742-6540-9

Library of Congress Cataloging-in-Publication Data
A catalog record for this book is available from the Library of Congress.

Typeset by Mark Heslington Ltd, Scarborough, North Yorkshire

Sabrina Mahfouz

Chef

For my son

Cast

Chef, *Jade Anouka*

Creative Team

Writer – Sabrina Mahfouz
Director – Kirsty Patrick Ward
Designer – Fran Reidy
Lighting Designer – Douglas Green
Sound Designer – Edward Lewis
Produced by Just For Laughs Theatricals
CEO – Adam Blanshay
Chairman – Gilbert Rozon
Assistant Producer – Missy Thompson
General Manager – Tim Johanson

Director – Kirsty Patrick Ward

Director: *Chef* (Fringe First Winner/Underbelly, Edinburgh Festival 2014), *Evita* (MT4Youth/Belfast), *Comets* (Latitude/Festival No. 6), *People Like Us* (Pleasance), *Snow White* (Old Vic/Educational Tour), *Chavs* (Lyric Hammersmith/Latitude), *Present Tense* (Live Theatre), *Brave New Worlds* (Soho Theatre), *Life Support* (York Theatre Royal), Old Vic New Voices 24 Hour Plays 2011 (Old Vic).

Associate Director: *Communicating Doors* (Menier Chocolate Factory), Theatre Uncut Flagship Tour 2014 (Soho/regional tour), *Symphony* (Watch This Space, National Theatre/Lyric Hammersmith/Latitude Festival), *Young Pretender* (Edinburgh Festival 2011/Hull Truck/Watford Palace).

Assistant Director: *Othello* (Shakespeare's Globe), *Arcadia* (English Touring Theatre), *King Lear* (Shakespeare's Globe), The International Actors Fellowship (Shakespeare's Globe), *Our New Girl* (Bush), *Bunny* (Fringe First Winner, Edinburgh Festival 2010/regional tour 2011), *The Boy on the Swing* (Arcola)

Performer – Jade Anouka

Theatre includes: *The Vote*, *Henry IV* (Donmar), *Chef* (Edinburgh Festival), *Omeros* (Sam Wanamaker), *Julius Caesar* (Donmar and St. Ann's Warehouse, New York), *Clean* (Traverse & 59E59, New York), *Romeo and Juliet* (Shakespeare's Globe/UAE tour), *Moon on a Rainbow Shawl* (National), *Hamlet* (Shakespeare's Globe/European tour), *Romeo and Juliet* (Bolton Octagon), *Wild Horses* (Theatre503), *Love's Labour's Lost* (Shakespeare's Globe/US tour), *Blood Wedding* (Southwark Playhouse), *Twelfth Night* (York Theatre Royal), *The Merchant of Venice*, *The Taming of the Shrew* (RSC), *Dick Whittington*, *Golden Boy* (Greenwich), *Handa's Suprise* (Little Angel), *UnStoned*, *Outright Terror Bold*, *Brilliant* (Soho).

Film includes: *A Running Jump* (dir. Mike Leigh), *A Summer Hamlet*, *The Dark Channel*.

Television includes: *Doctor Who*, *Shakespeare Uncovered*, *Secrets and Words*, *Law & Order: UK*, *USS Constellation*.

Writer – Sabrina Mahfouz

Sabrina writes plays, poems, TV shows and articles. She was shortlisted for the 2015 Arts Foundation Award for Performance Poetry and in 2014 her show *Chef* won a Fringe First Award at the Edinburgh Festival. In 2013 her play *Clean* was produced by Traverse Theatre and transferred to New York, and she received a Sky Arts Scholarship Award for poetry, enabling her to write and produce *Chef* and a number of other works. She has also won an Old Vic New Voices Underbelly Edinburgh Award 2012 for her play *One Hour Only*; a UK Young Artists Award; a nomination for The Stage Award 2011 for her solo show *Dry Ice*; an Old Vic New Voices TS Eliot Award and a Westminster Prize for New Playwrights for her first short play, *That Boy*.

Her new play, *With a Little Bit of Luck*, will be produced by Paines Plough this summer and she is writing a TV series for Sky.

Her collection of plays and poems, *The Clean Collection*, is also available from Bloomsbury Methuen Drama.

Lighting Designer – Douglas Green

Theatre includes: Theatre Uncut 2014 and *The Bread and the Beer* (Soho and UK tours), *Step Live* (Saddlers Wells), *A New Play for the General Election* and *Laburnum Grove* (Finborough), *The Dreamer Examines His Pillow* (Old Red Lion), *Opera in the Gardens* (Chiswick House), *SOLD* (Pleasance Forth), *Songs for a New World* (Bridewell), *Sweeney Todd* (Rose)

Fashion and corporate theatre include: Vivienne Westwood Red Label, Richard Nicoll (London Fashion Week SS15). With IMAGINATION: 'Rolls-Royce Closed Room Tour and Launch of RR6 (private residency in Beverly Hills and world tour), Global Launch of the Jaguar XE (London Eye/the Thames), Land Rover Discovery Sport Gobal Debut (the Seine, Paris), 'Canon at Photokina 2014' (Cologne Messe) and booths and launches for various automotive brands at the New York, Los Angeles, Toronto, Detroit, Washington, DC, Brussels, Paris, Moscow, Delhi, Saudi, Shanghai, Beijing and Busan International Motor Shows.

As Associate/Assistant: *Don Giovani*, *Don Quixote* (Royal Opera House), *Privacy*, *The Physicists* (Donmar), *4000 Miles* (Bath Theatre Royal).

Douglas trained at the Central School of Speech and Drama.

www.douglasgreendesign.co.uk

Sound Designer – Edward Lewis

Edward studied Music at Oxford University and subsequently trained as a composer and sound designer at the Bournemouth Media School. He works in theatre, film, television and radio. He has recently been nominated for several Off West End Theatre Awards, and films he has recently worked on have won several awards at the LA International Film Festival and Filmstock International Film Festival.

Most recent credits include: *Hannah* (Unicorn), *The Cement Garden* (VAULT Festival), *The Speed Twins* (Riverside Studios), *Eugenie Grandet* (Hartshorn-Hook Productions), *Cuddles* (Ovalhouse), *Molly Sweeney* (The Print Room/Lyric, Belfast), *Ignorance* (Hampstead), *Gravity* (Birmingham Rep), *A Midsummer Night's Dream* (Almeida), *Thom Pain* (Print Room).

Producer – Adam Blanshay

Just For Laughs Theatricals is a subsidiary of Just For Laughs, the largest comedy producer in the world.

London credits include: *Kinky Boots* (Adelphi), *The Nether* (Duke of York's), *Sunny Afternoon* (Harold Pinter), *Made in Dagenham* (Adelphi), *Forbidden Broadway* (Vaudeville), *The Importance of Being Earnest* (Harold Pinter), *The Pajama Game* (Shaftesbury), *1984* (Playhouse), *Dirty Rotten Scoundrels* (Savoy), *I Can't Sing!* (London Palladium), *Ghost Stories* (Arts),

Ghosts (Trafalgar Studios – Olivier Award), *Mojo* (Harold Pinter), *In the Next Room or The Vibrator Play* (St James), *Perfect Nonsense* (Duke of York's/UK tour – Olivier Award), *Chimerica* (Harold Pinter – Olivier Award), *The Ladykillers* (Vaudeville), *Merrily We Roll Along* (Pinter – Olivier Award), *A Chorus Line* (London Palladium), *Old Times* (Harold Pinter), *Twelfth Night*, *Richard III* (Apollo), *A Chorus of Disapproval* (Pinter), *Abigail's Party* (Wyndham's/UK tour) and *Without You* and *Pippin* (Menier Chocolate Factory).

UK tour: *The Producers; The King's Speech, Hairspray, Shrek the Musical.*

Broadway credits include: *Wolf Hall, Living on Love, The River, The Curious Incident of the Dog in the Night-Time, The Cripple of Inishmaan, Bullets Over Broadway, Rocky, Twelfth Night/Richard III, Kinky Boots* (2013 Tony Award for Best Musical), *Evita, Jesus Christ Superstar, On a Clear Day You Can See Forever, Jerusalem, Catch Me If You Can, How to Succeed in Business Without Really Trying* and *The Scottsboro Boys*.

US tour: *Kinky Boots, Evita, Pippin.*

Toronto: *Kinky Boots.* Australia: *Matilda the Musical.*

www.hahaha.com

General Manager – Tim Johanson

Theatre includes: *Yellow Face* (National), *White & Red* (workshop), *United We Stand* (workshop), *Wingman* (Soho), *Port Authority* (Southwark), *The President and the Pakistani* (Waterloo East), *Miss Havisham's Expectations* (Trafalgar Studios), *Mirror Teeth* (Finborough), *Dirty Great Love Story* (59e59, New York), *Superjohn* (Firehouse Creative Productions, Edinburgh Fringe and tour).

Set Designer – Fran Reidy

Francesca is a graduate of RADA's postgraduate Theatre Design course.

Design credits include: *The Summer Book* (Unicorn Theatre), *Venice Preserv'd* (Spectator's Guild), *Visitors* (Up in Arms), *Amygdala* (Print Room), *Godchild* (Hampstead Theatre Downstairs), *Tommy* (Prince Edward/Pure) *The President and the Pakistani* (Waterloo East); *Sunset Baby* (Gate Theatre); *One Hour Only* (Old Vic New Voices Edinburgh); *Step 9(of 12)* (Trafalgar Studios); *Port Authority* (Southwark Playhouse); *Phaedra* (Cockpit Theatre) *Arab Spring,* (Arch 61), *The Shape of Things* (Gallery Soho); *BOOTY* (Only Connect). For RADA: *Our Town, Splendour* (GBS Theatre). She has recently production and costume designed the set and costumes for *Spring in June* for the London Film Academy. As Assistant Designer: *The Crucible* (Vanbrugh, designer Ben Stones).

She is the Associate Designer for Rhapsody of Words, The Helsingor Sewing Club and Troupe Theatre company. She is one of the Jerwood Young Designers for 2012.

This work was written and developed with the support of a Sky Academy Arts Scholarship and the assistance of Arts Council England.

Huge thanks also goes to the following, without whom *Chef* would have been near-impossible: Sky Arts, Peter De Haan, IdeasTap, The Hospital Club, Ollie Dabbous.

Chef

1

Chef *is wearing a white chef's top and jogging bottoms.*

She is the only actor and can be any age and any ethnicity.

She is writing 'The perfect peach' onto a whiteboard.

She lifts a large, cut, dripping peach and holds it out to the audience.

This here, yeh, this is a peach.
A ripe and ready to eat beautiful bit
of meaty peach flesh.
Now listen, right.
If you'd never tasted a peach before –
even like, a metally mouthed one
from a Basics tin or the kind ya find
binded in plastic for lunchboxes or some shit –
then when you finally put this peach
inside your cakehole you would be like,
WOW!
How the fuck did you make that, Chef?
And I could go on, couldn't I?
About how I mixed this ingredient
from an island with a long name,
with another one that was scavenged
from a motorway
not far away from where you was born
and marinated it for a year,
or some such bullshit. But I won't.
Cos I ain't made it, have I?
Life has made it. Mother Earth.
So why hurt perfection?
Why shake it about with flashes of flour
and sparks of sugar,
trying to make it look like a bit of puke
after a good night out?
I mean, what is that about?

Chef

Keep it as it is. A bleeding peach.
Just make it the best bleeding peach it can be.
Soak it in its own juice overnight.
Make sure you buy the right ones in the first place.
Organic and that, fresh, you know, no pesticides
or flies finding their homes in its furry fleshy skin.
Put your face right up to its glow and let it know
that you will love it, respect it,
think about how it grew,
before you smash it in your mouth
and munch it quicker than a junkie chick
on a shotter's dick.
But don't be all poncy prick about it,
like you know things no one else could ever know
about this dear sweet little peachy poo.
Cos after all,
a bit later on you'll be saying a 'see you later on'
to it all down the shitter.

Yeh, so that's my, shall we say – philosophy.
On the way I like to do my food, for my guests.
I don't want them to have to guess
what went into what's going into them.
I just do it plain and simple
but so good they never forget it.
Come back every day like they need it to live.
Cos here, they kinda do.
I give a little bit of myself every day to them,
a gift to my loyal guests.
Not literally, obviously,
I mean I don't chop a bit of pinky finger into the pot
or sprinkle dandruff on top of a stew –
let me tell you I ain't got that, by the way,
dandruff, that's proper rough.
I mean, I give from the inside.
Yeh. Trust me, I even got some tough women crying
from what I can do with a lettuce leaf.
As soon as they get that green between their teeth . . .

4

Well, it's all over.
Who needs diets when veg can taste that good?

This place I'm at now,
they aren't so keen for me to proper experiment,
which is all I want.
All I want really,
it's all I,
it's all that's keeping me going really.
The dream that one day
I'll be able to cook again my way.
Everyone just wants to cook their own way, you know?
And I sometimes think,
you know I used to think it a lot,
when some cocksucker was complaining
about it being too hot
or not hot enough
or it's a bit salty
it's not as fresh as I like
It's got too much sauce,
bit too dry
thought this wasn't fried
are you sure this is organic?
Where are the sides?
Is this all we get?
Haven't you got better bread?
The menu said the menu said the menu said –
FUCK OFF!
I used to think, do you know what this does,
this life?
It cooks. It feeds. It delivers. It delights.
Then it dies.
People just sit there,
take the plate in front of them,
pick at it,
lick the side of a spoon.
Feel no way about pooling groups
of unwanted food

Chef

together at the edges
and when it comes back,
where do you think it goes?
We see it,
we see them.
Bulging black bags heaving
with life sustenance that has been rejected,
like the time from my life it took to prepare it
never really mattered.
Like the farmer, the lorry driver, the packer,
like none of us even matter.
How much do you think –
do you think we matter?
Us sorry lot who somehow grow food
or make it palatable,
make it something edible?

Pause. **Chef** *smiles.*

Incredible innit, food?
Couldn't live without it.
But gone so quick,
so unceremoniously.
I think that's why I got into it,
cooking,
eating,
something to put love into
that you don't expect to stick around.
You know it will be gone soon.
Knowing is much much better than hoping,
than supposing.
Knowing it will be gone as soon as it's done,
there's something very comforting about that.
Something comforting about shiny clean surfaces too.
The silver makes me feel safe.
Clean, ya know? I'm very clean, me.
I need to feel cleaner than usual today.
Yesterday,
well something happened here

yesterday,
before dinner service . . .
It was a mess.
I saw the blood.
I didn't make it, it wasn't me, it wasn't mine . . .
I just saw it,
I tried to stop it, stem it,
I wiped it I tried to wipe it – I . . .

Chef

2

I loved a man once
who cut shapes into skin cos his words didn't work.
Worst thing was I worked with words,
making up lines for menus, writing reviews for food.
And so when I spoke he looked at me
like I'd hurt a part of him I'd never heard.
I never saw him do it, his work.
But I saw the blood, I wiped it,
dried like a dye-poisoned lake
from the leather of a jacket.
I scrubbed silver Prada trainers doused in DNA
with a bleach-dipped toothbrush
that he'd hardly used.
He wasn't used to a girl like me, he'd say,
Babes, you're so gully you know.
But proper clever too, you wanna do proper things innit?
And I'd smile like yeh, I know, you're right.
Even though every night I used to lie awake,
wonder what the fuck I was gonna do with my life.
Wasn't making enough money writing about food,
I sold some weed here and there but no big thing.
He said he'd bring me in to his shit if I really wanted
but he never did.
He just let me silently do what I always did.
Stroll through the netted smoke he blew,
wrap my legs around his hips and kiss
like my life depended on it.
Cos it sort of did.
If I had actually seen him do it, his work,
maybe I would have left.
Unable to handle the careless mess,
faces like smashed birthday cakes on the pavement.
But then again, maybe I wouldn't.
Because he was sexy and strong
and he made me feel like I was too.
When you've grown up

in a darkness so black it's blue,
that's not something to be taken lightly.
So when one night when he asked me,
Babes, can you put this down your shoe for me yeh?
I say yeh, minor, I was gonna wear boots anyway.
We drive away and I close my eyes,
making my mind as wannabe unsee-through
as the tinted windows on the rented car
that cost more than his flat –
but it was part of all that and he had to have it.
Just like I had to have him, needed him to be happy.
I needed him, to be happy.
After all, this was a world
where a girl could apparently never compete,
the shapes we'd cut into skin
would apparently be too neat,
we'd apparently feel sick
when it really came down to it,
hearing frozen branches of bones crack,
we wouldn't be able to handle that,
wouldn't have that 'thing' it takes
to scrape an eyeball with the edge of a blade
like it's some kind of food's unwanted skin,
bring a knee to a nose, a gun to a tied tongue.
We apparently
just wanted Alize mixed with champagne
and fun wrapped in wraps that never let us forget
who was boss,
how much it cost,
how hard it all was,
to live like this.
We wouldn't want to get our lips bust
because we needed to be looked at
like we were needed to be kissed
and he needed me to feel like this
so that I would need him,
help him feel less empty.
An emptiness that left him so full of soullessness

Chef

that he took his own life every night,
There's plenty of ways to die and still stay alive, babes
he used to say.
Anyway, this one night when my Gucci cowboy boots
were full of lead end dreams,
sharp angles that dug into my ankles
making me walk like I had one foot on the moon,
this one night I was standing by a nightclub door,
a loaded gun tucked into my sock
and I spied the possibilities of what I might do.
Like stop a bullet making spirals
through the wiry hair of his chest
by jumping up high,
slow motion hand in action
trigger pulled
but skin cold
as from across the room a bullet pierces me,
making shapes inside no man could make
no matter how much his words didn't work.
And I would die
and he'd be safe, unhurt
and I would die.
I wanted that a little bit, maybe a lot, I'm not sure.
But that isn't what happened at all.
I stood by the nightclub door and I thought,
how does it get to this?
How do kids who want to be astronauts and writers
and singers and engineers end up here?
In the dark corners of someone else's dream,
guarded by thick doors and clipboards,
playing with guns and fists and knives,
forgetting what it was like to be alive once?
They knew once,
before crunches of a system
made them feel that their minds were missing
that nobody would miss them,
that they were dismissed then
from living the type of life others lived . . .

2

But they would never be forgiven
for not dying trying to live like them.
When
was it ever even possible for us to live like them?

I bent down to get the gun out, ready to say,
I'm out let's duck out,
let's use our money start some sort of business,
it can still be illegal – just not this.
Not violence and conflict,
unpicking the bits of skin that makes up a person,
their memories their existence their reason for being.
Before my hand reaches in,
I see him.
My eye caught a mirror that showed me my life
and it wasn't looking too nice because there he was,
his hand on some girl's face as she faced
the stairs she was going down
and as he turned back around
and saw me looking
his look looked deeper
than if he'd just tried to deny he was inside her,
even though his dick was still in it as he said it.

I left the gun on the desk behind the door,
where the woman on the till
glanced down at it soundlessly
and then straight back to her magazine,
which was screaming about overweight faces
and racist footballers who they'd still marry anyway,
everyone says some things sometimes
that they don't mean, don't they?
I asked her for a pen and she smiled at that,
handed me a black biro. I never gave it back.

I went and sat at the back of a little Chinese place.
Late night type people,
picking their way through Peking duck rolls,
not looking like the night

Chef

was worth the extra crow's lines
their eyes would show them in the morning.
I started scribbling a menu
on the back of the crap red napkin.
I thought about the fried food I'd just ate,
that I'd paid for and hated.
I made up some late night convenient dishes,
fresh, simple.
Ran to the 24-hour Asda and made them all at home.
Called my bestie Annie, she came round for breakfast
to taste my late night snacks and she rubbed my back
as I spiced the food with a few tears,
telling me it was the best fucking meal she'd had in years.
She might have just been being nice,
as best mates do when you tell them
the love of your life is a complete prick.
I needed to hear it.
Later on a receptionist at a nice little bistro
near my little flat said the very same thing,
made me come in with samples for the chef
and imagine, he took me on,
taught me to make the things
I'd only written about before.

The chef was a kind man, a family man,
definitely not much of the type of man
I'd had in my life up till then,
his heart as golden as the lemongrass syrup he made.
As soon as I got in there at 7 a.m.
he would take his A4 notepad,
make eight sections in which to break down
into white lined boxes the dish I was learning that day,
explaining the secrets of its complex simplicity to me.
I was in awe of him –
except he didn't believe in baking,
which made my mum tell me to be wary of him.
I was disappointed too,
because baking is what had got me into it all

in the first place as a kid,
seeing that transformation.
Eggs, flour, sugar, butter one minute
and a cake the next.
Something so magical about that.
Whatever you do to meat, it's still meat, isn't it?

I learnt how to taste as if my tongue was a paintbrush.
I never gave up,
Chef liked my dedication, determination.
He was getting older by the hour, as we all are,
but his old had started to bend his bones.
He was looking forward to more time off he said,
he thought I was ready, he said.
Ready for what? I said,
I'm not,
I'm definitely not . . .
what?!
It had been four years, me and him, happy.
Now here I was, my own kitchen to run.
Scary, yeh, but maybe one step away,
maybe a decade away from owning my own place.
Insane to think this could really happen!
It *was* happening to someone like me.
I mean, wow.

Chef

3

Chef *wipes the previous words off the whiteboard and writes
'Coconut Curried Tofu' on it.*

I miss the taste of coconut.
Scraping it from the shell
felt like hard work that then deserved
the melting of that wet white meat
between teeth and oh, I loved it.
We don't ever get coconut in here.
But this recipe is to keep dreams alive,
for those who will write it down, memorise.
Then when they get out, they'll cook it at home
for all of those that haven't abandoned them.
I decided to write this recipe book in here
to keep my creativity flowing,
even when faced with the grim ingredients provided.
I've carved out a little corner in this kitchen where I have –

She pauses.

Where I *did* have my own two trainees, Sasha and . . .
Candice. And I get – got a bit of freedom.
But no tofu or coconut.
I reckon with this book here I'm creating,
even just writing these recipes down,
well, it makes life taste better,
the air seems scented with possibility.
Or it did.

Today they asked me to cook egg fried rice,
something nice to keep you all calm on a day like this.
I nodded my head,
cos when they ask what they mean is
that's what you'll do,
regardless of what menu has been planned for weeks.
So I do. Or I will do. Soon.
They said I have to wait to find out . . .
Find out if I'm staying here or being moved,

being investigated, about what happened to –
Candice.
The egg fried rice. I'll do it soon.
I don't know what the fuck they reckon is calming
about egg fried rice though.
Grease and pieces of memories of plastic takeaway boxes
that most of these women got
with their boyfriends on weekends,
the end of the week that usually ended with an ending
that would end your faith in humanity –
like with my Annie, for example.
Every Friday after work she would pick up
boxes of gloop from the local Chinese,
breeze through the door all kisses
and stockings covering knees that were expected
to spend an unreasonable amount of time on the floor.
After he got what he needed the food would be left uneaten,
noodles gloomily looking through foggy containers
at a scene of all too common domestic distress,
chunks of sweet and sour chicken solidifying
under the soundwaves of unextraordinary anger
directed towards the one
that was supposed to be the one that's loved.
Unloved black bean sauce sighing into itself
as fists vibrate worktops
and walls and doors and air and floors
and finally flesh always flesh,
sometimes bone,
then fist and bone would moan together
and tears would fall
and tissues would become the litmus test of
how much do you really love –
I really love
I really do
I'm sorry you know I
you know I wouldn't do
it's just that
you know that

Chef

the way you
the way I –
and the night is packed away into a black bin bag,
tagged with a *Let's not talk of that again,*
tomorrow will be better and maybe
we should just get pizza.

4

Chef *wipes the previous title off the board and writes*
'Yellowtail sashimi (on shaved turnip with rhubarb gravy)'.

Sashimi was my favourite out there.
I used to shave a turnip,
cover a marinated slab of rose petal pink raw fish with it,
cushioned with juice from a rhubarb and oh my god,
it tasted like heaven.
I imagine it as I write it down.
I do a lot of that. Imagining.
I imagine my restaurant, when I get out.
It's going to be industrial chic. You know the type.
Exposed brick, bare lightbulbs
with unenvironmentally friendly
but unbelievably more beautiful glowing filaments.
Concrete floors,
waiting staff who take orders without notepads
and know everything there is to know about the menu
and the menu – oh!
There will be pickled cucumbers
compressed into octagonals,
origami pastrami pastry,
cod cheeks and celery,
exquisite mash with gravy
and soup that is never soup but always broth,
chilled broth –
like with avocado tomato and fig
because I really hate
the taste of hot liquid on my tongue.
The taste buds don't deserve to be burnt
and my memories of hot soup
aren't ones I want to pass on . . .

Chef

5

The first time I felt the heat of soup on my skin
I was working on a sailboat in the Shetland Islands.
Was the first time I'd been in charge of a kitchen, too.

My dad was an army man, an angry man,
definitely not much of a family man.
Moved to the lower arctic middle bit of fucking nowhere
to grow salmon in a farm and smoke it.
Then one summer out of nowhere he invites me
to sail the north seas with him.
Mum wasn't too keen on letting me go,
he'd left her with not much more than a reshaped nose
and scars that would make sure he was always around
even when he hadn't eaten a meal with us for five years.
But I was sixteen and far from sweet.
I wanted to piss her off and also to get off the estate,
go somewhere that spat superiority at the local park.
So I went up there with a backpack,
oilskins and rubber boots.
Things I'd never be seen dead wearing in my high street,
but on the high seas things were different,
leaving land, paint pot houses on a cloudy canvas.
Fog that looks so cosy setting in,
strong wind making my hair sing
as loud as shipping forecasts
in staccato Scottish harmonies.
I shivered to the sound of barnacled propellers
and the deep laughs of *don't tell 'er indoors*
that bobbed from bunk to deck
as they told jokes I didn't get
and put up posters of women they'd never met.

I used to just smile and stay on the side,
steer the boat sometimes, stare a lot.
I'd never been in love
but I decided that I'd know when I was
because the man would remind me of the way

seagulls glide out of stalactite clouds,
suddenly,
smoothly,
that's how he'd find me.
A kid's dreams.

My dad knew how I liked to cook,
always helping whoever was doing it,
adding my own ingredients,
making meals taste the way fresh air does
when your window's been closed all night
and the sweat has stuck to your duvet.
The crew felt free when they ate my food they said,
thought only of the present, bit like meditation,
not that we'd do that hippy shit,
but you get it, Chef, don't ya?
I did, kinda,
though I was too ecstatic at being called 'Chef'
to bother figuring out the metaphor.
Dad swore excitedly
and handed the kitchen galley over to me.
I thought I'd scored, he was doing me a first ever favour,
realising later it was the thing they all hated to do the most.
That day I cut veg as the boat swayed,
the edge of the blunt blade bit my thumb,
bit of blood on the onions,
no big deal,
blue plaster on,
carry on.
Served up thick, hot soup in cups, buttered bread.
Made my way up the stairs
only one cup,
one slice at a time.
Fine, swaying but okay.
Good balance from days spent on a skateboard as a kid.
Waves drip their blue beards over the deck,
I get up and down four times
and it's the last step up,

Chef

the cup in my hand,
the bread sitting on its rim,
the handle's heat softening my forefinger's cuticle.
Then Trident or Jupiter or Mars or Ares
lurches at the boat
with the fury of a Friday night closing time
after production line lay-offs
and off I went – over my ankle
trip
quick
flick of the toe
can't grip
slip slip slip
soup flicks
orange bits everywhere
hair stuck sticky steam –

You stupid dumb fuckin bitch what's wrong with you
can't even carry some stupid cups of fucking soup
fucking useless you int ya
little shit
I should throw you in that cunting sea
see see see
see what I can do to you
see what I mean
you stupid dumb –

he strangled and strangled me
until I couldn't breathe.
Like my neck was a winch
his fingers becoming the lengths of rope
that oxoxoxoxoed over and over again.
His eyes awash with waves
of his own dad's whisky skin,
until one bloke stepped forward
with a wet cloth,
Don't worry boss,
I'll mop that up.
Just like that Dad forgot

to keep doing those things to my skin
that made me remember
what it was like to have him as a live-in father.
I jumped off at the next harbour
and didn't cook again for five years.

Chef

6

Chef *wipes the previous title from the board and writes*
'Red wine risotto (with mushroom marmalade)'.

I try and find the ones in here
who have a knack with the food.
They come and train with me.
I'm strict, demanding, but fair, I think.
No shouting,
in a well-run kitchen there's no need for shouting.
No Gordon Ramsaying round here.
There's two main deputies after me.
Sasha, she deals with scrubbing the veg,
but her very best speciality is mushrooms.
She don't say much,
but she knows how to make amazing mushroom sauce
and she smiles a lot. I've got her back.
Then there is, there was,
Candice . . .
Good at mashing and with rolling pin things,
plus she sings sweeter than Manuka honey on iced mango
so I love to have her around.
When I'm feeling a little low a little slow,
her voice speeds me up,
makes me remember that it's good to be alive,
isn't it?
Even just a little bit,
even if sometimes it feels like
why would you want to be alive
when you're holed up here?
We met on my first day,
You ain't gonna last long with them books in ya arms,
she said.
I showed her pictures of food in the cookbooks I held
and her whole face changed,
became quiet and soft like misplaced compliments.
Later on, she told me when other inmates stole stock,
she lent me socks when mine had holes in,

6

she made me laugh when nobody came to see me.
Oh Candice . . .
Who sings sweeter than Manuka honey on iced mango.
You know, there's such a sad story behind the melodies,
I suppose there usually is.
When she was a kid her mum had an affair
with her dad's dad and so her dad
attacked his dad with an axe
until every bit of his cheating brains had been spat out,
then went round to his own house,
stuck a hose down his wife's throat
until she bloated so full of water she pretty much burst
and then he ran to the railway at the back of the garden,
flung himself onto the tracks in front of a cargo train
that didn't even stop as pieces of his flesh
spotted all the leaves on all the trees all around the tracks.
Candice . . .
Well she saw all of that.
Not the axe bit but the rest of it.
She was just a kid, nine or ten.
No mum or dad or granddad.
A grandma who tried her best but died
when Candice was fourteen, so she went to homes
and was one of many
who got groomed into becoming girls
who do things for boys
who will never be men.
It's a miracle really that she hadn't killed anybody,
she just got caught trying to steal a microwave from Currys
which when you think about what she's been through,
I mean who gives two tosses about a bloody microwave?
But this judge did for some reason,
maybe he was breathing rotten air that day
or had given up smoking or was trying to make a point
about stealing being wrong when you live in a place so right?
Who knows?
She came in here and tried to take her own life
in a whole host of imaginative ways.

23

Chef

Each time a quick stay in the medical ward,
another pop into the psych rooms,
which were full of women who were being marked down
as just having a 'strange turn'
because the officials didn't want
suicide attempts counted up by governments
who might take away budgets, bids, contracts even.
When I heard about it all, the lengths she went to,
I thought this girl needs some responsibility,
some purpose, so I had some words with the governor,
a man called Dave,
okay, give her a permanent kitchen position
but don't let her near the knives!
Sign here and here to prove I've said what I've said
and good luck, Chef.

I put her on mashing duty.
Taught her how to make
the best potatoes or turnip or celeriac,
or whatever other root I can convince them to provide,
at just the right consistency using only peelers, mashers
and if cutting was required she passed it on.
I was keeping my promise, my responsibility.
She seemed to like the sounds of the kitchen,
metallic rhythms mixed with her saccharine tones.
When she felt like letting loose
I would come in on the chorus
and Sasha would just nod along.
So we were cool in there,
we're alright, we're fine,
getting through our time one day at a time.
That's what I'd say to her and then –

She pauses.

They said they can't tell us anything.
Not even me.
It's like a huge secret.
I mean we saw her bleeding,

I stepped in her blood,
I was in her blood.
I mean she was just there right there,
I just asked how she was,
then she said all that . . . stuff.
I'd just said,
hey Candice how are you doing?
She turned on me and usually
I would never be there like that with it in my hand,
usually I'd never be near her with anything
she could use like that,
I signed I promised I knew –
but maybe I was thinking of something else
or maybe I wanted to test her . . .
No, no that's not what I wanted to do,
definitely not, she was, she is the best one here.
It's. Shit . . .
The way her wrist just flicked the knife from my hand
so dextrously, so delicately
until she – then it –
the bleeding was so deep I couldn't breathe.
She didn't speak it was so quick,
I screamed they came quick,
I flipped tea towels over the cut,
tripped on the blood,
it stuck to my apron to my nose to my shoes
and I swear she laughed.
I have a bruise now, a big bruise.
They took a picture, said they might need it for future,
for future evidence, in case there was a case,
in case I was involved somehow.
I'm like how,
how could I have been involved
she's my girl, she's my girl
I never did anything!
Yeh, yeh,
that's something we've never heard, Chef.
Don't worry yourself sure it will be fine,

Chef

she's unlikely to die, it looked deeper than it was.
This time you probably won't get the blame,
be a shame if you did, we know you liked that kid,
but you know how it goes.
It don't look great you got her blood on your nose
and the knives are locked up, it's only you with the key
and you signed you signed and Dave said
you know she's your responsibility
it's your responsibility –

7

Mum said I didn't have a good sense of responsibility.
That what happened was in one way or the other
because of me, I should just accept it.
She did.

Dad had a hard time of it in the salmon-farming business.
Even the fish thought he was a dick,
didn't want to be around him either.
First sniff of a sea change related infection
and they were like 'yeh, see you later',
took it on and dropped,
floated up to the top.
Let's remember
he was an army man, an angry man
definitely not much of a family man.
Mum said he had seen deaths undeserved
on the side of the road
and maybe he had killed.
I thought he had definitely killed.
His eyes had that capability to reflect
everything he was seeing so it never really had to go in,
defence mechanism for those who do things
beyond vision, beyond retelling.
Imagine something so bad it could never be retold,
that's the look his whole being owned.
I always hoped he hadn't passed it on to me.

The fish died.
I never got to ask him,
but I guess that made him think about his own death,
the blood and guts mess he'd made of his life.
So he came to London, to find me, my mum,
apologise, start a new life with new lies.

I was closing up, mid-week quiet night.
There was mud on his boots,
it hadn't rained for a while.
He stood there

like he should be there,
as if he could never be unwelcome.
There wasn't one bit of his bobbled skin
that I wanted to let in,
this was my kitchen,
my fucking kitchen,
his boots his mud his muck wasn't welcome.
Come in, he said,
can I come in?
I ignored him.
It was late,
I was cleaning,
scrubbing silver to lake-lit moonlight,
the last night before the first night off in ten days.
Swaying with tiredness,
the tonelessness of his voice
fighting with the memory I had of its bite.
What for,
what do you wanna come in for?
I didn't even look up,
kept scrubbing,
wiping.
See,
I want to see you.
I'm here, you've seen.
What do you want from me?
Nothing, I want nothing.
You should leave.
I need you to see me.
I won't look.
Wiping still, I wonder if my cooking
will be spoilt by this intrusion,
will this memory infuse all my soft fruits,
plait itself into my pastry?
Just leave me and my kitchen.
I let you run your first one.
Bullshit.
On the ship, I did.

Yeh, then you tried to twist all the breath outta me,
leave me be.
I'm not giving in.
Go. You're too slow.
It's all over, no daughter for you.
If you don't let me,
I mean it's all that's keeping me going really,
it's all I want, it's all I –
don't give a shit.

Now I look.
He's got broken eyes
and a starry heart stuck in thunderclouds.
The sight makes my soul quiet but my voice loud
and I shout.
Now you ain't proud?
You wanna come to love me,
come to get loved by me?
See where I am? Do you see?
There will be a Michelin star on this window.
I cook here, create here,
make here be as much of life as I can
because outside of this
I'm not safe,
I don't know the way.
Your way was where you went
and there wasn't any space there for me.
You bring flesh and blood to air
and expect it to what?
Live without love for so long that it moulds its own,
saving all that for the day you decide to come back?
My life has been made up of days waiting
to discover darker parts of myself.
Digging inside skin until I can pull out
exactly what is so bad about me that makes everyone leave,
believing that those parts are the markings
that map the outlines of my life,
of who I can be

Chef

and so of course off I go to find those
that stretch that, scratch that
tell me to forget that,
those thoughts are of no importance
based in no truth whatsoever –
but then do you know what they do?
Of course you do cos it's what you did,
what you do.
Everyone fucking leaves.
So I will not mend your broken eyes
with stitches of moisture
from my soaked-through scrapbook.
No, no, that's not me,
that's not who you made.
This is the last thing I'll ever say to you,
who threw my limbs into circuses of swimming pools
never teaching me to swim,
painting only hell into the word 'him',
please, Dad, just fucking leave.

And he did.
And there was that sinking part of me
that wanted him to refuse,
to use his helicopter voice,
cut through the density of pre-dawn London
and tell me no,
I will stay here until you let me speak with you,
about things that those who come
from someone's insides should probably at least try out.
Like, what TV shows do you watch?
Do you get to go out much? Did you study?
Who broke your heart? Did you cry?
What song do you want played when you've died?

But there was none of that.
Just the back of an old man,
leaving one last time.

A few months later I was round Mum's for Sunday dinner.
She liked to cook for me in front of her friends,
so she could say,
See, even the famous local chef can't say no to my roasties!
And it's true, they were the best,
I always took my own gravy though.
When everyone had left that day she told me,
Your dad's dying you know,
he's not got long.
Oh.
I don't want to talk about –
Everyone deserves a bit of forgiveness.
He got a bit.

Two years went past.
The phone rang,
he was raspy on the other end, no anger now,
quiet.
I can't leave the flat anymore.
I've got you on speakerphone because I can't hold it anymore.
At night time when there's no carer,
I get stuck in the toilet and I sleep there,
in my shit, bathroom floor cool on my skin.
They will take me to a home soon,
I've never had a home, I won't go.
He had not one person in the world,
he wanted to pass away,
stop being a burden to himself,
to the memories of everyone else.
He knew it was a lot to ask,
but he thought I might enjoy it,
do us both the biggest favour.
He had it all figured out,
he wanted me to inject a lethal dose of something into him
so it worked quicker, nicer.
He'd be gone so quick, so nice.
I said, how can I do that, Dad?
The phone dropped, went dead.

Chef

I went round, picked it up for him.
Against my better judgement yes,
but when I saw him so helpless
I felt –

*(This memory of the past is now interspersed with more recent
questioning about Candice.
As the scene progresses, in amongst reliving the court trial she faced
for her dad's murder, in which she was found guilty, she is also faced
with the questioning from prison officials over Candice's apparent
suicide.)*

Glad,
maybe you were glad when Candice asked you for help,
like your dad did?
Maybe this is it, you've found your calling,
helping people who want to die, die.
Although you can never prove they wanted to, can you?
No, no my calling is cooking.
Take a look at my CV it's clear for whoever wishes to see.
What exactly did she say to you?
She said,
the grey here creates a never-ending hurricane of dust
inside her mind.
I want to find the sea.
Will you help me?
I just said, 'How you doing, Candice?'
And that's what she said, she asked me to help her.
To find the sea?
Metaphorically.
You knew what she meant?
I knew what she meant, yes.
She was looking for death to lap up
the inconsequence of this existence.
She had tried so many times,
always got it wrong, got everything wrong.
You're the closest thing I've ever had to a friend, Chef.
She wanted me to help her go,
like she said she knew I'd done with him.

I said 'no, no, no'.
I would never do that,
I had never done that with him, they were wrong,
she was wrong, I had never done that. I –

Of course the fingerprints were mine,
it was my knife,
my kitchen,
it was in my hand,
she took it,
I'm telling you she took it,
have a look at her history,
her history isn't pretty,
she wanted to die.
She did.

* He did,
what's it got to do with me?
He wanted to die.
Check his history,
his history ain't pretty.
Domestic violence, PTSD
Iraq, fish farms,
rings all the alarms.
Do you accept that you didn't like your father much?
We accept that he didn't appear to like you.
Beat you, left you,
one time it looks like you almost died.
Can't have been nice, can it?
Can it?
We, the prosecution, put forward that revenge is a clear motive.
The defendant wanted her father dead,
using his disability
as a cover-up for her premeditated murder –
Objection!
Do you care at all what I have to say?
It wasn't me.
He wanted to die cos he lived a crap life.
He was a terrible example of a man and yes,

Chef

he's dead. Yes, I wanted him out of my life
but that doesn't mean I needed him to die.
Well we, and we venture the jury too,
wholeheartedly disagree.
Goodbye.

8

Chef *wipes the previous title off the board and writes*
'Red berries with hibiscus jasmine sorbet'.

It can be messy this one.
Red berries.
They're very soft,
leave trails of their sweet insides on the plate
if you don't treat them delicately enough.
They're everyone's favourite,
even when they're not real,
'Give me the red one pleeease!'
We used to shout for fruit gums, Opal Fruits,
whatever, those things with no fruit in them whatsoever.
The sorbet is difficult but delicious.
I wouldn't say it's for the amateurs,
but I'm hoping
that those who get to this point in the book
have a certain amount of skill
and most importantly determination.
For the sorbet, you will need eggs, caster sugar,
jasmine tea leaves and hibiscus flowers –
fresh, if possible.
Candice said her favourite drink was hibiscus tea.
Strange as she struck me as a PG Tips girl,
but you can never tell really, can you?

She died, they said.
Fatal penetrating injury to the lower left quadrant of the chest,
suggesting she aimed for the heart.
She missed, she always did.
The knife perforated the lower lobe of her left lung,
causing traumatic internal bleeding.
She must have grabbed your hand extremely hard
for the angle to remain at a lateral aspect
but we guess she was determined.
And between you and me,
we would far rather deal with a suicide fine

Chef

than get marked down with murder in the annual report,
nobody wants that, do they?

She would have loved a little sorbet
flavoured with her favourite tea flower.
Doesn't taste too sweet too soapy, just right for sorbet.
Just right for summer days.

When you put the berries on the plate
use a clean spoon for each one,
be gentle,
their red insides,
so sweet.
Don't let them creep onto the plate.
It's up to whoever eats the dish to decide
if the berries go inside the sorbet
or stay divided –
give them the choice.
There should always be a choice,
shouldn't there?